# Crabapples

# Big trucks, big wheels

Petrina Gentile ✪ Bobbie Kalman ✪ Marc Crabtree

🌳 Crabtree Publishing Company

# Crabapples

## created by Bobbie Kalman

**Per i miei genitori Giovanna e Petito.
Vi ringrazio per la vostra pazienza e il vostro amore.**

**Editor-in-Chief**
Bobbie Kalman

**Writing team**
Petrina Gentile
Bobbie Kalman

**Managing editor**
Lynda Hale

**Editors**
Niki Walker
Greg Nickles

**Computer design**
Robert MacGregor
Lynda Hale
Lucy DeFazio

**Color separations and film**
Dot 'n Line Image Inc.

**Printer**
Worzalla Publishing Company

**Special thanks to**
The parents and children who assisted with photo shoots including
Pat, Danielle, Peter, and Jordan Gentile; Ross, Amanda, and Allison
Vernal; Connie Warner; Krista, Jamie, and Jenna Braniff; Marianne,
Paul, and Michael Alfonsi; Maryanne, Jasmine, and Corey Book; Ralph
Natale; Osia Wilson; Meagan and Jaimee Grove; Marty Palleshi and
Husky Truck Stop; Scott D. Johnston of BIGFOOT 4x4 Inc.; Deputy
Chief Bill Osborn, Platoon Chief Bob Gill, and the St. Catharines Fire
Department; Dan Leger, Bill Braybrook, and Dave Borris of Niagara
Hydro; Todd Beam, Larry Loosemoer, and Stoney Creek Furniture;
Norman Hope and George Ermanson of Niagara Fruit & Vegetable
Growers Ltd.; Dick Hyatt of Niagara Hospital; and the big rig truck
drivers including John Comfort, Paul Gambel, Scott McPherson,
Robert Millard, Bill Book, Tony Ledda, and Jim Grove

**Photographs**
All photographs by Marc Crabtree except the following:
Petrina Gentile: page 4 (bottom)
David and Beverly Huntoon: pages 4 (top), 10
Scott D. Johnston/BIGFOOT 4x4 Inc.: pages 10-11
Diane Payton Majumdar: pages 12, 14 (both), 15 (both)

## Crabtree Publishing Company

| 350 Fifth Avenue | 360 York Road, RR 4, | 73 Lime Walk |
| Suite 3308 | Niagara-on-the-Lake, | Headington |
| New York | Ontario, Canada | Oxford OX3 7AD |
| N.Y. 10118 | L0S 1J0 | United Kingdom |

**Cataloging in Publication Data**
Gentile, Petrina, 1969-
    Big trucks, big wheels

(Crabapples)
Includes index.

ISBN 0-86505-642-0 (library bound)   ISBN 0-86505-742-7 (pbk.)
Big rigs, monster trucks, and emergency vehicles are among
the types of trucks discussed in this book.

1. Trucks - Juvenile literature.  I. Kalman, Bobbie.  II. Title.
III. Series: Kalman, Bobbie. Crabapples.

TL230.15.G46 1997        j629.224        LC 97-4091
                                                CIP

# What is in this book?

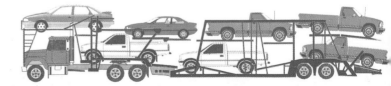

# Trucks are everywhere!

Trucks do all kinds of tough work. Some are used to fix things high above the ground. Some move things from factories to stores. Others are needed to fight fires. What other jobs do trucks do?

In this book you will see children near trucks, but you should never play near trucks. It is dangerous! When these pictures were taken, adults were nearby to make sure no one got hurt.

# Parts of a big wheel

Big trucks do not all look alike. They come in many shapes and sizes. The truck below is called a **big rig**. Look at the different parts on this truck. Not all trucks have these parts.

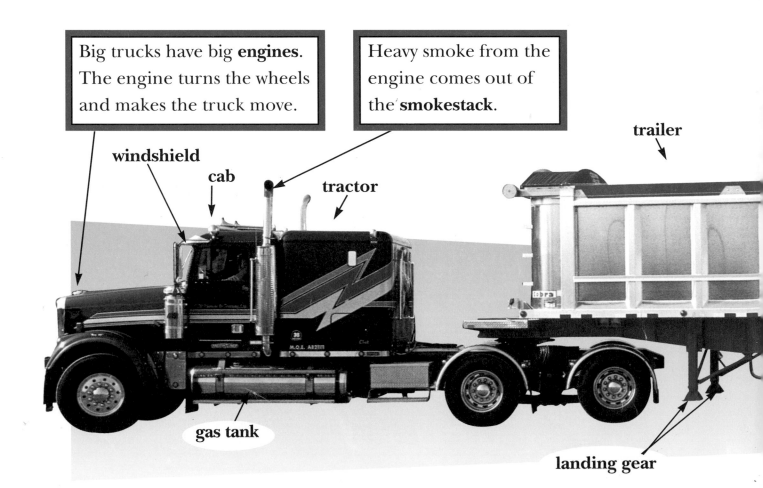

Big trucks have big **engines**. The engine turns the wheels and makes the truck move.

Heavy smoke from the engine comes out of the **smokestack**.

**windshield**

**cab**

**tractor**

**trailer**

**gas tank**

**landing gear**

The driver sits in the **cab**. He or she turns the large steering wheel to move the truck left or right.

Trucks that drive long distances have a bed behind the seat. The driver sleeps here during a trip.

Some trucks have more than 20 wheels! How many wheels do you see on this one? How many are hidden?

A **4x4** is a pickup truck that has four-wheel drive. A truck with four-wheel drive is powerful. The engine turns all four wheels instead of just two. A 4x4 can easily drive up hills and through snow!

Some 4x4s have an open area behind the cab. It is called a **box**. The box is handy for carrying all kinds of stuff. You can load it with camping gear, bicycles, dirt bikes, or toboggans.

# Monster machines!

A **monster truck** is like a 4x4, but its tires are much bigger. It also has more parts. A monster truck does not come from the factory in one piece. Its owner puts it together one part at a time. That is why no two monster trucks are the same.

Monster trucks drive over old cars for fun. They crush the cars in seconds! The drivers must be careful. A truck can tip over if one of the cars under it moves. Many drivers flatten the tires of the cars so the cars do not move when the monster truck drives over them.

# Dumpers

**Dump trucks** are used to build roads and buildings. They have a big, open box for carrying heavy loads. This box is called a **dumper**. Dumpers can hold lots of dirt, rocks, and gravel.

Big **treads** help the tire move easily over bumpy ground.

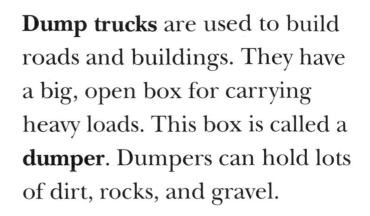

Michael, on the right, is taking a look at all the dirt inside this dumper. When it is time to dump the load, the driver makes sure no one is behind the truck. Then the driver tilts up the dumper, and the load comes pouring out!

# Cleaners

A **garbage truck** moves trash. Garbage is thrown into the large opening at the back of the truck. This opening is called a **hopper**. Garbage is squeezed together inside the hopper. When the truck is full, the driver takes it to a **landfill**, or garbage dump. The hopper is raised, and the trash tumbles out!

ST. CATHARINES
WASTE COLLECTION
SERVICE
988-3RRR

16

A **recycling truck** moves things that can be recycled. It has many different sections, or **buckets**, along its side. Glass, cans, plastics, and newspapers go into these buckets. Cardboard is put into the back of the truck. When the truck is full, the driver takes it to a recycling plant. The driver empties one bucket at a time.

Don't let their name fool you—
**wreckers** do not wreck things.
They pull, or **tow**, cars that have
broken down. They also tow cars
that have been in an accident.
Wreckers are also called tow trucks.

1 This wrecker is very strong.
It can tow away heavy trucks such
as big rigs and monster trucks.

tow bar

2 The driver pulls the switch, or **lever**. The **crane** moves down and toward the front of the wrecked truck.

3 The **tow bar** at the end of the crane attaches to the front of the wrecked truck. The wrecker then tows away the big truck.

# Emergency trucks

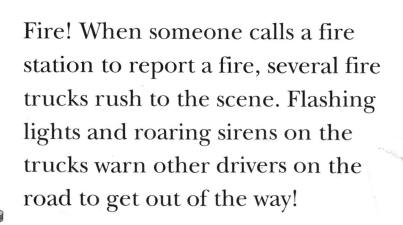

Fire! When someone calls a fire station to report a fire, several fire trucks rush to the scene. Flashing lights and roaring sirens on the trucks warn other drivers on the road to get out of the way!

There are many kinds of fire trucks. Each one has a different job. A **pumper truck** carries hoses and water to put out the fire. It also pumps water from a hydrant. Three or four hoses can be attached to the back of the truck. The driver controls how much water comes gushing out of each hose.

The ladder on an **aerial-ladder truck** helps firefighters reach fires high up in buildings. The driver raises and lowers the ladder. The **outrigger legs**, below, help keep the truck steady when a firefighter climbs the ladder.

20

An ambulance is like a small hospital on wheels. It carries bandages, medicines, and a stretcher to accidents and fires. It moves people who are hurt to the hospital. The back doors open wide so the stretcher can be pushed in or pulled out easily.

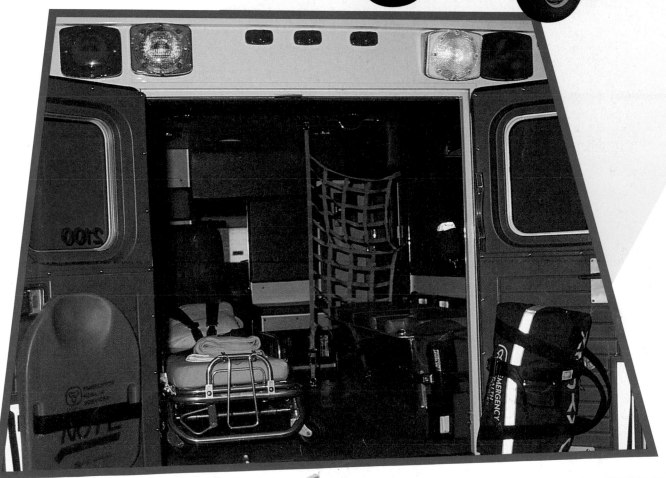

# Big rigs

A big rig is a truck with two parts—a **tractor** and **trailer**. The tractor has the engine and cab. The trailer is the part that carries the load.

Some people call big rigs **tractor-trailers** or **combination trucks**. They are also called 18-wheelers because most big rigs have ten wheels on the tractor and eight wheels on the trailer.

## Connecting the trailer

A tractor attaches to a trailer with a **fifth wheel**. The fifth wheel is shown above. It is not really a wheel. It is the part on the back of a tractor that locks onto a trailer.

The driver connects **lines** from the tractor to the trailer. The lines control the brakes to stop the trailer. They also make the trailer's lights work.

# Types of trailers

Tractors pull many kinds of trailers. The most common trailer is a **dry van**. A dry van looks like a large box. It is used to carry toys, books, stoves, and many other things.

This dry van is used to deliver furniture. The furniture is covered with lots of blankets. It is also tied to the walls to keep it from sliding around. If the furniture slides from side to side in the truck, it could get scratched and broken.

A **flatbed** trailer has no walls or roof.
It carries cargo that is too large or
heavy to move in and out of a dry
van. Sometimes a crane is used to
load concrete blocks or other heavy
things onto a flatbed. Thick ropes
or chains hold the load in place.
The metal wall at the front of a
flatbed is called a **bulkhead**. It stops
a load from crashing into the cab
when the truck stops quickly.

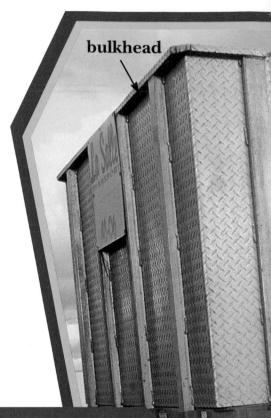

bulkhead

**Car carriers** move cars and trucks. They can move ten cars or trucks at once! The cars and trucks are chained so they will not roll off the car carrier. Car carriers have two levels. When the bottom level is empty, the top level is lowered to drive cars and trucks on and off it.

A **tanker** moves liquids such as gasoline, milk, pop, and juice. When a tanker is full, it holds more liquid than 200 bathtubs!

A special code on the tanker shows what type of liquid is in the tank. The code is shown on the side and back of the truck. The tanker on the left has the code 1791, which means it is carrying a dangerous liquid called acid.

# Picture glossary & index

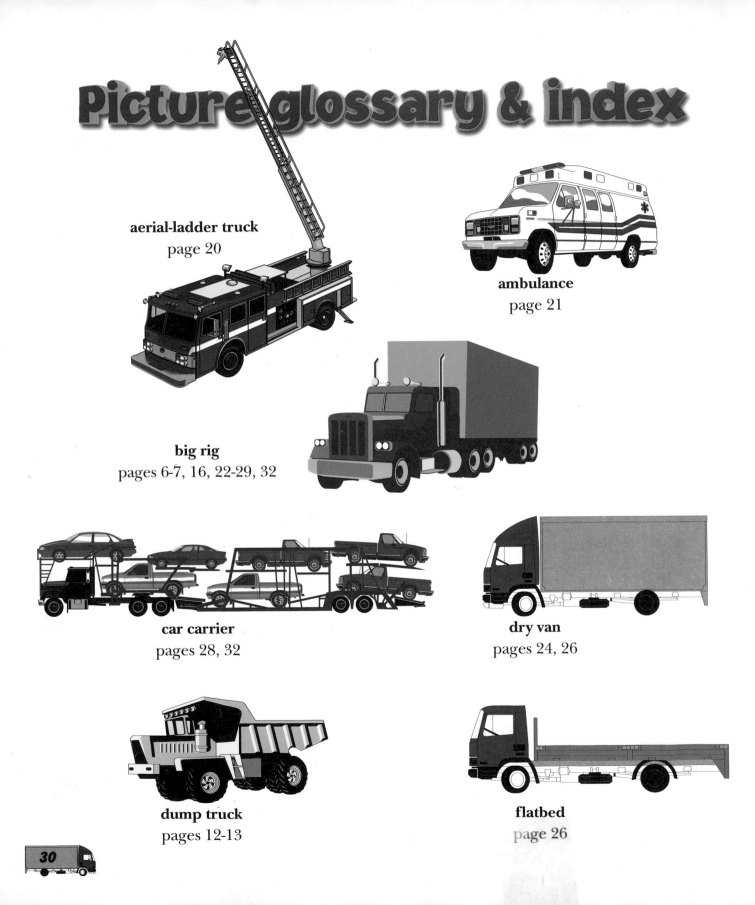

**aerial-ladder truck**
page 20

**ambulance**
page 21

**big rig**
pages 6-7, 16, 22-29, 32

**car carrier**
pages 28, 32

**dry van**
pages 24, 26

**dump truck**
pages 12-13

**flatbed**
page 26

**4x4**

pages 8-9, 10

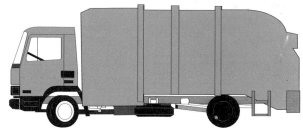

**garbage truck**

page 14

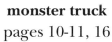

**monster truck**

pages 10-11, 16

**pumper truck**

page 19

**recycling truck**

page 15

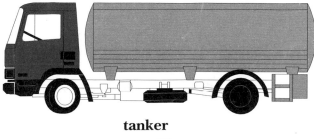

**tanker**

page 29

**wrecker** or **tow truck**

pages 16-17, 32

**31**

# Truck talk

Some big trucks have a CB radio. Drivers use their CB radio to make emergency calls. They also use them to talk to other drivers when they are driving alone.

Allison is practicing her truck talk with a big-rig driver miles away. She uses special words that only a big-rig driver knows. Here are some of those words.

**back down**—slow down
**bobtail**—to drive a tractor without a trailer attached
**bubble machine**—a police car with lights on its roof
**bubblegummers**—children
**coffee pot**—a restaurant
**convoy**—trucks driving in a line
**draggin' wagon**—a tow truck
**gearjammer**—a person who drives a truck for a living
**hole in the wall**—a tunnel
**nap trap**—somewhere to stop to rest or sleep
**pedal pusher**—a bicycle rider
**portable parking lot**—a car carrier
**pumpkin**—a flat tire
**ratchet jaw**—a CBer who talks on the radio a lot
**roller skate**—a small car
**set it down**—stop quickly
**winkin' blinkin'**—a school bus

3 4 5 6 7 8 9 0 Printed in USA 6 5 4 3 2 1 0 9 8